AF840804

AI Payroll, Sales Tax & Employer Compliance

How Algorithms Prevent Penalties & Late Filings

By Joe Correa

Published by Live Stronger Faster

This book is for educational and informational purposes only. The author and publisher are not engaged in rendering legal, financial, tax, or other professional advice. Readers should consult a qualified professional before making any financial decisions.

First Edition

Table of Contents

Introduction

In the modern business world, nothing drains profits faster, causes more stress, or creates greater legal exposure than payroll mistakes, sales tax errors, and employer compliance failures. Unlike income tax, which is typically filed once per year, payroll and sales taxes are relentless. They are due weekly, bi-weekly, monthly, quarterly, and annually, with hundreds of different rules, thresholds, deadlines, and agencies involved. A single missed payroll deposit, a late sales tax filing, or an incorrectly classified employee can trigger cascading penalties, interest, audits, and even criminal liability. For decades, these obligations have been handled through a patchwork of accountants, bookkeepers, payroll services, and manual processes that were slow, expensive, and prone to human error. Artificial intelligence changes that forever. In this book, you will discover how AI now serves as the invisible compliance engine behind modern businesses, automatically tracking, calculating, filing, and reconciling payroll taxes, sales taxes, and employer obligations with a level of precision, speed, and reliability that no human system can match.

Payroll is not just about paying employees; it is a highly regulated tax system disguised as a payment process. Every paycheck contains federal income tax, Social Security, Medicare, state income tax, unemployment insurance, workers' compensation, and often local taxes, all of which must be calculated correctly, withheld, deposited on strict schedules, and reported to multiple agencies. Add to this the complexity of overtime rules, tipped employees, commissions, bonuses, benefits, retirement contributions, and multi-state payroll, and it becomes clear why payroll is one of the most error-prone areas of any business. Traditional payroll systems rely on static tables and manual inputs that struggle to keep up with constantly changing tax laws and labor regulations. AI-driven payroll platforms, however, continuously update themselves with new tax rates, thresholds, and legal rules, automatically applying them to every employee in real time. Instead of reacting to compliance problems after they occur, AI prevents them before they ever happen.

Sales tax is even more complex than payroll. With the rise of e-commerce, digital products, subscription businesses, and online marketplaces, companies are now exposed to sales tax obligations in dozens or even hundreds of jurisdictions. Every state, county, and city can set its own tax rates, exemptions, filing schedules, and reporting formats. A business selling software, digital courses, physical goods, or services online may trigger sales tax nexus in multiple states without even realizing it. Failing to register, collect, or remit sales tax correctly can lead to massive back taxes, penalties, and audits that can destroy a growing company. AI-powered sales tax engines continuously monitor transactions, customer locations, product categories, and nexus thresholds, automatically determining when and where tax must be collected and remitted. What once required a team of tax specialists can now be handled by algorithms in milliseconds.

Employer compliance extends far beyond payroll and sales tax. Businesses must comply with labor laws, minimum wage requirements, overtime regulations, health insurance mandates, workers' compensation coverage, unemployment filings, immigration verification, and countless reporting obligations. Each employee creates a legal and financial footprint that must be tracked and managed across multiple government agencies. Historically, these requirements were handled through spreadsheets, paper files, and disconnected software systems that left businesses vulnerable to mistakes and audits. AI now unifies all of these obligations into a single compliance intelligence layer, ensuring that every employee, every hour worked, and every dollar paid is properly documented, classified, and reported.

One of the most powerful advantages of AI in payroll and compliance is its ability to operate in real time. Instead of waiting until the end of the month or quarter to discover errors, AI continuously audits payroll runs, tax calculations, and filings as they occur. It flags anomalies, detects misclassifications, and alerts businesses to potential compliance risks before they turn into costly violations. This proactive approach transforms compliance from a reactive burden into a predictive, preventative system that protects cash flow and business continuity.

Another major breakthrough is the way AI integrates payroll, sales tax, and accounting into a single financial truth. In traditional systems, payroll lives in one platform, sales tax in another, and accounting in a third, requiring constant reconciliation and manual adjustments. AI connects all of these data streams automatically. Every paycheck, every tax deposit, and every sales transaction flows directly into the company's financial records in real time, creating a continuously accurate ledger. This not only simplifies bookkeeping and tax preparation but also gives business owners and CFOs an always-up-to-date view of their true financial position.

For growing businesses, multi-state operations are where compliance complexity explodes. Hiring remote employees, selling across state lines, or operating in multiple jurisdictions introduces new tax registrations, filing requirements, and labor laws. AI platforms are designed to scale with this complexity. When a business hires an employee in a new state, the system automatically registers the company with the appropriate agencies, applies the correct tax rules, and begins filing the required reports. When sales expand into new markets, AI detects the nexus and adjusts tax collection accordingly. What once required weeks of legal and accounting work can now happen automatically in the background.

Risk reduction is one of the most overlooked benefits of AI-driven compliance. Government agencies are increasingly using their own AI systems to detect payroll fraud, sales tax evasion, and misclassification of workers. Businesses that rely on manual processes are at a growing disadvantage because their errors are easy for government algorithms to find. AI-powered businesses, on the other hand, operate with the same level of precision and data integrity as the agencies that regulate them. This creates a powerful defensive shield against audits, penalties, and enforcement actions.

This book will show you how to design an AI-powered payroll and tax compliance stack that works 24/7 without human intervention. You will learn how AI classifies workers correctly as employees or contractors, calculates payroll taxes with perfect accuracy, files forms automatically, and ensures every deadline is met. You will see how sales tax automation platforms determine nexus, apply the correct tax rates, generate filings, and remit payments across hundreds of jurisdictions. You will also learn how employer compliance systems manage labor laws, benefits, and reporting so that your business remains legally protected as it grows.

More importantly, you will discover how these systems free business owners from the fear and friction of compliance. Instead of worrying about penalties, audits, and government letters, you gain confidence that your business is operating inside a continuously updated legal and tax framework. This allows you to focus on growth, innovation, and profitability while AI quietly handles the most dangerous and complex parts of business operations.

AI payroll and compliance is not about replacing accountants or payroll professionals; it is about elevating them. By automating the repetitive, error-prone tasks, AI allows financial professionals to focus on strategy, optimization, and advisory work that actually increases profits. Businesses that adopt AI early gain a massive advantage over competitors still trapped in manual systems and fragmented software.

As you move through this book, you will begin to see payroll, sales tax, and employer compliance not as burdens but as systems that can be optimized for efficiency, accuracy, and financial control. Artificial intelligence transforms these obligations from sources of risk into engines of stability and growth. In the AI-powered business, every paycheck strengthens compliance, every sale is tax-optimized, and every employee is managed within a perfectly documented legal framework.

This is the future of business operations: invisible, automated, and mathematically precise. And in the pages ahead, you will learn how to build it.

Chapter 1

The AI Compliance Engine: How Payroll, Sales Tax, and Employment Rules Became Automated

Modern businesses no longer fail because of bad ideas or poor products; they fail because of compliance breakdowns. Missed payroll deposits, incorrect sales tax filings, misclassified workers, and late government reports quietly bleed companies until cash flow collapses or regulators step in. For decades, compliance was treated as an unavoidable cost of doing business, something to be handled manually by bookkeepers, accountants, and payroll clerks who relied on outdated tables, disconnected systems, and human memory. Artificial intelligence has now transformed compliance into an automated operating system that works continuously in the background of every transaction, paycheck, and invoice, enforcing tax law with machine precision while eliminating the human error that used to create risk.

The AI compliance engine is not a single piece of software but a layered ecosystem of algorithms that watch, calculate, verify, and report everything a business does in real time. When an employee clocks in, AI immediately begins tracking labor law compliance, overtime thresholds, benefit eligibility, and payroll tax exposure. When a customer places an order, AI determines whether sales tax applies, which jurisdiction it belongs to, and how much must be collected. When a paycheck is issued, AI calculates every withholding, schedules deposits to the correct agencies, and prepares the required forms. These processes run continuously, updating themselves as laws change, ensuring that businesses never fall behind regulatory requirements.

One of the greatest dangers in traditional payroll systems is their reliance on static tax tables and periodic updates. Tax laws change constantly, with new rates, thresholds, credits, and reporting rules introduced every year. Manual payroll systems only update when a human installs new software or enters new data, creating gaps where businesses unknowingly apply outdated rules. AI payroll engines, however, connect directly to tax authorities, regulatory databases, and compliance feeds, automatically updating themselves the moment a change occurs. This means that every paycheck is calculated using the most current law available, protecting businesses from penalties caused by outdated information.

Sales tax compliance is even more complex because it depends on geography, product type, and economic nexus thresholds that vary by state and country. A single online sale can trigger tax obligations in multiple jurisdictions if the business crosses revenue or transaction limits. AI systems continuously monitor sales volume, customer locations, and product classifications, determining when nexus is established and automatically registering the business with the appropriate tax authorities. Instead of discovering tax liabilities months or years later during an audit, AI ensures compliance is enforced at the moment each sale occurs.

Employer compliance goes far beyond payroll taxes. Businesses must follow wage laws, overtime rules, health insurance mandates, unemployment insurance regulations, immigration verification, and workplace safety requirements. AI-powered human resources platforms integrate with payroll and accounting systems to create a unified compliance record for every employee. Every hour worked, benefit provided, and tax withheld is logged and verified against legal requirements, creating a continuously updated compliance audit trail. This protects businesses not only from tax agencies but also from labor disputes, lawsuits, and regulatory investigations.

Another critical function of AI compliance systems is classification. One of the most common and expensive mistakes businesses make is misclassifying workers as independent contractors when they should be treated as employees. AI analyzes contracts, job duties, hours worked, and payment patterns to determine the correct classification under federal and state law. If a risk of misclassification appears, the system alerts the business before penalties accumulate. This proactive compliance is impossible in manual systems, where misclassification often goes unnoticed for years.

AI also transforms how businesses handle filings and payments. Instead of waiting until the end of the quarter to prepare payroll tax returns, sales tax reports, and employer filings, AI generates these forms continuously. When a filing deadline arrives, the reports are already complete, validated, and ready for submission. Payments are scheduled automatically, ensuring that taxes are deposited on time without human intervention. This eliminates late fees, interest, and the administrative burden of chasing deadlines.

From a financial perspective, AI compliance systems improve cash flow and forecasting. Because payroll taxes and sales taxes are calculated and reserved in real time, businesses always know how much of their cash belongs to the government and how much is truly available for operations. This prevents the common mistake of spending tax money that was supposed to be remitted later, a trap that has bankrupted countless companies. AI creates financial clarity by separating taxable funds from operational funds the moment revenue is earned. The true power of the AI compliance engine lies in its ability to scale. A business can grow from one employee to one thousand, from one state to fifty, and from one product to hundreds without increasing its compliance workload. AI simply expands its data processing and rule enforcement automatically. What once required an army of payroll clerks, tax specialists, and compliance officers is now handled by algorithms running quietly in the background.

As governments themselves increasingly use AI to detect fraud, underreporting, and compliance violations, businesses that do not adopt AI become easy targets. Their errors stand out against the clean data generated by automated systems. AI-powered businesses, on the other hand, operate with the same digital precision as the agencies that regulate them, making audits faster, easier, and less dangerous.

In this new world, payroll, sales tax, and employer compliance are no longer obstacles to growth. They become infrastructure, quietly supporting expansion while protecting profits. The AI compliance engine ensures that every dollar paid and every dollar collected is accounted for, every law is followed, and every filing is completed, allowing businesses to focus on innovation, strategy, and scale rather than paperwork and fear.

The Company That Never Missed a Deadline

When Daniel Reyes launched his digital marketing agency, he thought payroll would be simple. He had three freelancers, a few clients, and a steady stream of invoices. But within a year, his team had grown to twelve people scattered across five states, each with different tax rules, overtime laws, and reporting requirements. One missed payroll deposit triggered a penalty letter from the IRS, followed by a state labor notice, and suddenly Daniel was spending more time dealing with compliance than running his business. He felt like he was drowning in invisible rules that kept changing without warning.

Everything changed when Daniel implemented an AI-driven payroll and compliance platform. From the moment it went live, the system began analyzing every worker, every contract, and every payment. It immediately flagged two contractors who should legally be employees under state law, allowing Daniel to fix the classification before penalties could accumulate. It registered his business in two new states where he had unknowingly crossed sales tax nexus thresholds. What had once been hidden risks became visible, manageable, and controllable.

Each payday, the AI system calculated payroll taxes with precision, scheduling deposits to federal and state agencies automatically. Daniel no longer worried about missing deadlines or using the wrong tax rate. When one of his employees moved to a different state, the system adjusted her withholding, updated registrations, and generated new compliance forms without anyone lifting a finger. It felt like having a team of accountants, tax attorneys, and payroll specialists working around the clock.

Sales tax had been Daniel's biggest fear. His agency sold digital services and subscriptions nationwide, and he had no idea where he was supposed to collect tax. The AI platform tracked every sale, determined which jurisdictions required collection, and automatically added the correct tax to each invoice. At the end of the month, the system generated the required reports and submitted payments to each state. What once seemed impossible became routine.

When an audit notice finally arrived, Daniel was terrified—until he realized how different this time was. His AI system had already compiled every payroll record, tax filing, sales transaction, and compliance report into a perfectly organized digital file. The auditor reviewed the data, found everything accurate and complete, and closed the case in days instead of months. There were no penalties, no back taxes, and no surprises.

As Daniel's business continued to grow, he noticed something remarkable: compliance was no longer a bottleneck. He could hire anywhere, sell anywhere, and scale without fear. The AI compliance engine made his company feel invincible, protected by a digital shield that never slept and never forgot.

In a world where most businesses were still fighting spreadsheets and government forms, Daniel's company had become something different—a machine that followed every rule automatically, quietly, and perfectly. And that, he realized, was the true power of artificial intelligence in business.

Chapter 2

AI Payroll Intelligence: From Every Hour Worked to Every Dollar Reported

Payroll is the financial heartbeat of every business. It determines how employees are paid, how taxes are collected, and how governments monitor economic activity. Yet for decades payroll has been one of the most fragile systems inside companies, dependent on manual data entry, static tax tables, and human oversight. One small error—an incorrect overtime calculation, a missed tax deposit, or a misclassified worker—can trigger cascading penalties and regulatory scrutiny. Artificial intelligence has transformed payroll from a fragile administrative function into a real-time financial intelligence engine that connects labor, taxation, and compliance into a single automated system.

At the core of AI payroll is continuous data capture. Every hour worked, every bonus earned, every benefit applied, and every deduction taken is recorded and analyzed in real time. Instead of waiting for the end of a pay period to calculate wages, AI payroll systems track compensation as it happens. This allows them to immediately detect when overtime thresholds are reached, when minimum wage laws are being approached, or when benefit eligibility changes. By monitoring payroll dynamically, AI prevents violations before they occur rather than correcting them after damage has already been done.

Tax calculation is where AI delivers its greatest value. Payroll taxes involve federal, state, and local income taxes, Social Security, Medicare, unemployment insurance, and various special assessments. Each employee may be subject to different rules depending on their location, income level, and benefit elections. AI systems process these variables instantly, applying the correct tax rates and limits to every paycheck. Because these systems connect directly to tax authority databases, they always operate with the most current laws, eliminating the risk of using outdated tax tables that plague traditional payroll systems.

One of the most dangerous payroll risks for businesses is misclassification. Treating an employee as an independent contractor or vice versa affects tax withholding, benefits, and legal obligations. AI payroll platforms analyze work patterns, contracts, hours, and payment structures to determine whether a worker meets legal definitions under IRS and state labor laws. When a classification risk appears, the system alerts management before penalties and back taxes can accumulate. This predictive compliance is one of the most powerful ways AI protects businesses from regulatory disasters. Payroll also serves as a primary data source for financial planning. Because AI systems know exactly how much labor costs in real time, they allow businesses to forecast cash flow with unprecedented accuracy. Employers can see how upcoming payroll runs will impact bank balances, how tax deposits will affect liquidity, and how hiring decisions will change expenses. This turns payroll from a backward-looking record into a forward-looking financial control system.

AI payroll also integrates directly with benefits administration, including health insurance, retirement plans, and paid time off. Every benefit deduction is calculated automatically, applied to the correct employee, and reported to providers. Compliance with benefit mandates such as the Affordable Care Act is monitored continuously, ensuring that coverage thresholds and reporting requirements are met. This eliminates the manual reconciliation that often leads to compliance gaps and employee disputes.

When payroll data flows into accounting systems automatically, businesses gain a real-time view of labor costs across departments, projects, and locations. AI categorizes wages, taxes, and benefits into the correct accounts, creating a continuously accurate general ledger. This eliminates the need for monthly payroll journal entries and reduces the risk of financial statement errors. Auditors, investors, and lenders gain access to clean, reliable data that reflects the true financial condition of the company. Another critical function of AI payroll is filing and reporting. Forms such as W-2s, W-3s, 941s, state wage reports, and unemployment filings are generated automatically based on live payroll data. When deadlines arrive, the forms are already complete and validated. Payments are transmitted electronically to the correct agencies, ensuring that nothing is late and nothing is forgotten. The entire payroll compliance cycle becomes a seamless, automated flow instead of a stressful scramble.

For businesses with remote and international employees, AI payroll becomes even more powerful. It can apply country-specific tax treaties, currency conversions, and reporting rules automatically, allowing companies to hire globally without building complex payroll infrastructure. What once required international accounting firms can now be handled by intelligent software that understands global labor law.

In this new AI-powered payroll world, paying people correctly and legally is no longer a burden. It becomes a competitive advantage. Companies that deploy payroll intelligence can scale faster, hire with confidence, and avoid the hidden costs that destroy so many growing businesses. Payroll is no longer just a cost; it is a controlled, optimized financial system that supports sustainable growth.

The Payroll That Never Lied

When Olivia Park launched her fast-growing software startup, she thought payroll would be the easiest part of running her company. After all, she only had a few engineers and designers at first. But as her product went viral, she hired across multiple states and even overseas. Suddenly, payroll became a maze of tax rates, benefit deductions, and compliance rules that no one fully understood. Each pay period felt like a gamble.

After a painful payroll tax penalty drained thousands of dollars from her bank account, Olivia implemented an AI payroll platform. The system immediately began analyzing her workforce. It flagged inconsistencies in overtime calculations, identified a misclassified contractor, and corrected benefit deductions that had been applied incorrectly. What she once paid accountants weeks to find was now revealed instantly.

Every payday became smooth and predictable. The AI system calculated wages, withheld taxes, and scheduled deposits automatically. Olivia could see her upcoming payroll and tax liabilities days in advance, allowing her to manage cash flow with confidence. When she hired a developer in another state, the system registered her company with the local tax agencies and updated withholding rules without any paperwork.

One day, a government auditor requested payroll records. Olivia simply exported the AI system's compliance log, which showed every calculation, every filing, and every payment in perfect order. The audit was closed in hours with no adjustments.

For the first time, Olivia realized that payroll no longer controlled her business. She controlled it. With AI watching every dollar and every hour, her company ran with mathematical precision, free from fear and full of possibility.

Chapter 3

AI Sales Tax Automation: How Every Transaction Becomes Instantly Compliant

Sales tax is one of the most misunderstood and underestimated risks in modern business. Unlike income tax, which is calculated once a year, sales tax is triggered by every transaction. Each time a customer buys a product or service, a new tax obligation is created, governed by complex rules that vary by state, county, city, and even by the type of product being sold. In a digital economy where businesses sell across borders, through websites, marketplaces, subscriptions, and mobile apps, sales tax exposure multiplies rapidly. Artificial intelligence has become the only practical way to manage this complexity at scale, transforming every transaction into a compliant, traceable, and correctly taxed event.

At the core of AI sales tax automation is jurisdiction intelligence. AI systems continuously analyze customer location data, IP addresses, shipping destinations, billing addresses, and digital delivery rules to determine which tax authority has the right to collect tax on a given sale. Unlike traditional systems that rely on static address tables, AI evaluates multiple data points and resolves conflicts automatically, ensuring that tax is applied to the correct jurisdiction even in ambiguous cases. This prevents both under-collection, which leads to audits and back taxes, and over-collection, which creates customer disputes and regulatory issues.

Product classification is another area where AI provides dramatic accuracy. Sales tax does not apply uniformly to all products. Food, software, digital services, clothing, and professional services may be taxed differently or exempt entirely depending on location. AI systems analyze product descriptions, SKUs, and transaction metadata to assign the correct tax category automatically. As tax laws change or new exemptions are introduced, the AI updates its classification logic, ensuring that businesses always apply the correct rules without manual reconfiguration.

Economic nexus rules have created one of the greatest compliance challenges in modern history. States now require businesses to collect sales tax once they exceed certain revenue or transaction thresholds, even if the business has no physical presence in that state. AI sales tax engines continuously monitor sales volumes and transaction counts by state, alerting businesses the moment they cross a nexus threshold. The system can then automatically initiate tax registration, begin tax collection, and prepare filings for the new jurisdiction. What once took months of discovery now happens instantly.

AI also automates exemption management. Many customers, such as resellers, nonprofits, and government entities, are exempt from sales tax. Managing exemption certificates manually is a nightmare of expired documents, missing files, and audit risk. AI systems store, verify, and monitor exemption certificates, applying them automatically when valid and alerting businesses when renewals are required. This ensures that exempt sales are handled correctly while maintaining a complete compliance audit trail.

When it comes time to file and remit sales tax, AI eliminates the chaos of multi-state reporting. Every transaction has already been categorized, taxed, and logged. The system aggregates this data into jurisdiction-specific reports that match the exact formats required by each tax authority. Payments are calculated and transmitted automatically. Instead of scrambling at the end of the month or quarter, businesses operate in a state of continuous readiness, with filings and payments always up to date.

From a financial perspective, AI sales tax systems create unprecedented transparency. Businesses can see exactly how much tax they have collected, how much they owe, and which jurisdictions are involved at any moment. This prevents the dangerous practice of spending sales tax money that belongs to the government. By segregating tax liabilities in real time, AI protects cash flow and prevents the accumulation of hidden debt.

As governments deploy their own AI systems to detect underreporting, AI-powered businesses gain a critical defensive advantage. Their transaction data is clean, structured, and consistent, making audits faster and less risky. Instead of fearing tax authorities, compliant businesses can demonstrate accuracy and transparency instantly.

In the AI-driven economy, sales tax is no longer a guessing game. Every transaction becomes a perfectly documented legal event, automatically aligned with the law. This transforms compliance from a threat into a controlled, automated system that supports growth instead of limiting it.

The Sale That Changed Everything

When Marcus Bennett opened his online electronics store, he focused on sourcing products and driving traffic. Sales poured in from across the country, and his revenue skyrocketed. But beneath the surface, a storm was building. He had no idea that many of those sales triggered tax obligations in states where he had never set foot. The warning came in the form of a thick envelope from a state tax agency demanding years of unpaid sales tax. Panic set in. Marcus realized that every sale he had celebrated might now cost him twice as much in penalties and interest.

Desperate, he implemented an AI sales tax platform. Within days, the system mapped every transaction he had ever made, identified where nexus existed, and calculated exactly what he owed. More importantly, it began collecting the correct tax on every new sale going forward. Customers saw accurate tax amounts on their invoices, and Marcus finally understood his true revenue.

When another state audit arrived months later, Marcus was ready. He provided detailed, AI-generated reports that showed every sale, every tax rate, and every payment. The auditor nodded, impressed by the precision.

For the first time, Marcus realized that growth without compliance was an illusion. With AI watching every sale, his business was no longer a ticking time bomb—it was a machine built to last.

Chapter 4

AI Employer Compliance: How Algorithms Enforce Labor Law, Benefits, and Workforce Regulations at Scale

Employer compliance is the most underestimated and misunderstood risk category in modern business. While payroll and sales tax errors create financial penalties, employer compliance failures can shut down operations entirely. Labor law violations, benefit noncompliance, improper worker classification, missing documentation, and reporting failures expose businesses to lawsuits, government enforcement actions, and reputational damage that cannot be undone with money alone. Historically, employer compliance has been handled through fragmented systems, manual HR processes, and institutional memory that disappears when employees leave. Artificial intelligence replaces this fragile framework with a continuously enforced compliance architecture that treats labor law as executable code rather than static policy.

At the foundation of AI employer compliance is rule interpretation. Labor laws are complex, layered, and frequently ambiguous, with federal, state, and local regulations overlapping in ways that even experienced professionals struggle to interpret. Minimum wage, overtime eligibility, meal and rest breaks, predictive scheduling, family leave, disability accommodations, and workplace safety rules all vary by jurisdiction and employee classification. AI systems ingest these laws directly from regulatory sources and convert them into machine-readable logic that can be enforced automatically. Instead of relying on training manuals or HR judgment calls, compliance becomes a real-time calculation applied to every employee interaction.

Worker classification is one of the most dangerous compliance zones for any business. Misclassifying employees as independent contractors can trigger years of back taxes, unpaid benefits, penalties, and legal exposure. AI compliance engines analyze multiple data points simultaneously, including hours worked, payment structure, job duties, managerial control, exclusivity, and contractual language. By comparing these factors against federal and state classification tests, AI determines the legally defensible classification for each worker. When risk thresholds are crossed, alerts are triggered before enforcement agencies ever get involved. This proactive defense is something manual systems cannot replicate.

Benefits compliance is another area where AI fundamentally changes outcomes. Health insurance mandates, retirement plan eligibility, paid leave requirements, and workers' compensation coverage are governed by strict rules tied to employee counts, hours worked, and company size. AI systems monitor eligibility continuously, ensuring that benefits are offered, withheld, and reported correctly. If workforce size crosses a regulatory threshold, the system adjusts benefit requirements automatically. Reporting obligations are generated without delay, eliminating the risk of accidental noncompliance caused by growth.

Documentation is the silent backbone of employer compliance. Every employee generates a trail of legally required records: hiring forms, tax documents, eligibility verification, timekeeping logs, performance records, benefit elections, and termination notices. Missing or incomplete documentation is one of the most common triggers for labor audits and lawsuits. AI systems create immutable, time-stamped compliance records that cannot be altered retroactively. Every action is logged, every form is stored, and every update is traceable, creating a defensible audit trail that protects the business in disputes.

Timekeeping and wage compliance are enforced automatically through AI monitoring. Overtime thresholds, break requirements, and scheduling rules are tracked continuously. If an employee is approaching a violation, the system can alert management or adjust schedules automatically. This prevents accidental violations that often occur when managers are unaware of labor law limits. Compliance shifts from correction to prevention, dramatically reducing exposure.

AI employer compliance systems also integrate with payroll, accounting, and legal reporting to create a unified workforce compliance ecosystem. Wage payments align perfectly with labor law calculations. Benefits deductions match eligibility rules. Tax filings reflect correct classifications. This eliminates the inconsistencies that regulators often use to identify noncompliant businesses.

As governments increasingly use AI to detect labor violations, businesses without automation become easy targets. Discrepancies between payroll, tax filings, benefits, and timekeeping are quickly flagged by enforcement algorithms. AI-powered businesses, however, generate consistent, verifiable data that aligns across systems. Audits become procedural rather than adversarial.

In the AI-driven enterprise, employer compliance is no longer a reactive HR function. It becomes a continuously enforced operating system that protects the company, employees, and leadership simultaneously. Businesses that adopt this model do not merely comply with labor law—they operationalize it, embedding legal integrity directly into daily operations.

The Lawsuit That Never Happened

Ethan Morales never thought of himself as reckless. He built his logistics company slowly, hiring drivers and warehouse staff as demand increased. At first, compliance seemed manageable. His HR manager kept files in cabinets, payroll was outsourced, and benefits were handled through emails and spreadsheets. Nothing felt urgent. Nothing felt dangerous. That illusion shattered the day a former employee filed a labor complaint.

The letter arrived without warning. It alleged unpaid overtime, improper classification, missing break periods, and benefits violations. Ethan's stomach dropped as he read the words. He replayed every decision in his head, wondering where things went wrong. His attorneys warned him that labor cases rarely hinge on intent. They hinge on documentation. And documentation, he discovered, was fragmented, incomplete, and inconsistent across systems.

Facing potential litigation that could bankrupt his company, Ethan made a decision that would change everything. He implemented an AI employer compliance platform, not knowing whether it could save him—but knowing that his old system could not. The AI immediately began ingesting years of workforce data, reconstructing employment histories, analyzing time records, payroll entries, and benefit enrollments with relentless precision.

Within days, the system identified compliance gaps Ethan had never known existed. Certain drivers had crossed overtime thresholds without proper documentation. Break logs were inconsistent. Contractor classifications in one state were legally indefensible. But instead of merely reporting these issues, the AI created a remediation plan. It corrected classifications, adjusted benefit eligibility, generated retroactive documentation where legally permissible, and flagged items requiring legal review.

More importantly, it changed how the company operated moving forward. Every shift was monitored. Every break was logged automatically. Every benefit threshold was enforced in real time. Managers received alerts before violations occurred. What once relied on human memory became enforced logic.

Months passed. The lawsuit never materialized. The employee withdrew the complaint after documentation was produced showing corrected classifications and payments. Regulators never followed up. The storm passed quietly.

As Ethan expanded into new states, the AI adjusted labor rules automatically. New hiring triggered updated compliance requirements. Growth no longer increased risk. It reduced it.

Years later, when another logistics firm collapsed under labor violations, Ethan understood what had saved him. It wasn't luck. It wasn't good intentions. It was infrastructure. While others treated compliance as paperwork, his company treated it as code.

And code, unlike people, never forgets.

Chapter 5

AI Filing, Reporting & Penalty Prevention: How Compliance Becomes Invisible and Automatic

The final failure point in payroll, sales tax, and employer compliance is not calculation—it is execution. Businesses rarely incur penalties because they did not owe taxes; they incur penalties because filings were late, forms were incomplete, payments were misapplied, or reports were submitted to the wrong agency. Compliance collapses not at the level of intention, but at the level of timing and coordination. Artificial intelligence fundamentally reshapes this problem by transforming filing and reporting into an automated, continuous process rather than a deadline-driven event.

Traditional compliance systems operate in cycles. Payroll is processed, then reported. Sales tax is collected, then reconciled. Employer filings are prepared weeks or months after the underlying activity occurred. Each step introduces delays, handoffs, and opportunities for error. AI eliminates these gaps by treating every transaction, paycheck, and workforce event as a real-time reporting input. Forms are not created at the end of a period; they are assembled incrementally, validated continuously, and finalized automatically when deadlines arrive.

At the core of AI-driven filing is pre-validation. Government forms are unforgiving. A single incorrect number, missing identifier, or formatting error can trigger rejection, penalties, or audits. AI systems validate every data point against filing rules long before submission. Taxpayer identification numbers, employee records, jurisdiction codes, and reporting thresholds are checked automatically. If an inconsistency appears, it is flagged immediately, allowing correction before submission rather than after rejection. This alone eliminates a massive percentage of compliance failures.

Timing is another critical advantage. AI systems maintain live calendars of federal, state, and local filing deadlines, adjusting automatically for holidays, jurisdiction-specific rules, and changes in filing frequency. Payments are scheduled with precision, ensuring that deposits arrive exactly when required—not early, not late. This prevents both penalties and unnecessary cash outflows. Businesses no longer need to remember deadlines because the system executes compliance autonomously.

One of the most dangerous compliance risks is misapplied payments. When taxes are paid manually, funds are often sent to the wrong agency, credited to the wrong period, or applied incorrectly within government systems. AI platforms track payment confirmations, reconcile agency receipts, and verify that funds were credited properly. If discrepancies occur, the system flags them immediately and initiates corrective actions. This closes a loophole that has historically caused businesses to owe taxes they already paid.

AI also transforms year-end reporting, which is traditionally one of the most stressful periods for employers. Forms such as W-2s, 1099s, and annual reconciliation reports are generated automatically from continuously verified data. Instead of scrambling to correct errors in January, businesses enter year-end with forms already complete, reconciled, and audit-ready. Employees and contractors receive accurate documents on time, reducing disputes and regulatory exposure.

Penalty prevention is not passive; it is predictive. AI compliance systems analyze patterns that historically lead to enforcement actions, such as inconsistent filings, unusual wage fluctuations, or deviations from industry norms. When risk indicators appear, the system alerts leadership before regulators do. This early warning capability allows businesses to correct course proactively rather than react defensively. Perhaps the most profound shift is psychological. When filing and reporting become invisible, businesses stop making decisions out of fear. Growth no longer feels dangerous. Hiring does not trigger anxiety. Expanding into new markets does not create compliance paralysis. AI removes the emotional tax of compliance by replacing uncertainty with mathematical certainty.

In the AI-powered enterprise, compliance does not happen because someone remembered to file a form. It happens because the system was designed to make noncompliance impossible. Filing becomes a background process, penalties become statistical anomalies, and regulatory risk fades into irrelevance. This is not incremental improvement—it is structural immunity.

The Letter That Never Came

For nearly a decade, Samantha Reed lived in quiet fear of the mailbox.

Every morning, she checked it with the same knot in her stomach, half-expecting an envelope with an unfamiliar government seal. Her manufacturing company had grown fast—faster than her systems. Payroll ran through one vendor, sales tax through another, and employer filings were handled by a rotating cast of accountants who each left behind a slightly different process. Nothing was technically "wrong," but nothing felt secure.

The first penalty came quietly. A late payroll filing. Then another, this time for sales tax in a state she barely remembered registering in. Each letter was small, but together they created a sense of inevitability. Samantha began making decisions defensively. She delayed hiring. She avoided new markets. Growth felt like danger disguised as opportunity.

The breaking point came when her controller resigned. In his exit interview, he admitted something she had suspected for years: no one fully understood the compliance system. It worked because people compensated for gaps with memory, emails, and improvisation. When people left, knowledge left with them.

Samantha realized she wasn't running a company—she was holding together a fragile compliance truce.

She implemented an AI compliance platform not because she believed in technology, but because she had run out of alternatives. The transition was uncomfortable. The system surfaced issues she didn't want to see: misapplied tax payments from years earlier, filing inconsistencies across states, reporting mismatches that had never been reconciled.

It was overwhelming—but different. For the first time, the problems were visible, structured, and solvable. The AI didn't just report issues. It resolved them. It contacted agencies electronically, corrected misapplied payments, aligned filings across periods, and rebuilt the company's compliance history into a single, coherent record. What once felt like a tangled past became a clean timeline.

Then something unexpected happened.

Nothing.

No letters arrived. No penalties followed. Filing deadlines passed without notice. Payments were executed silently. Reports were submitted automatically. Samantha stopped checking the mailbox obsessively. Weeks turned into months. Months into years.

When an expansion opportunity arose—three new states, dozens of new employees—she didn't hesitate. The AI registered jurisdictions automatically, adjusted filing schedules, and incorporated new rules without meetings or panic. Growth felt light for the first time.

One afternoon, a peer CEO mentioned a devastating audit that had nearly shut his company down. Samantha listened quietly, realizing something unsettling: she could no longer remember the last time she worried about compliance. The fear that once shaped every decision had evaporated, not because the rules disappeared, but because they were finally enforced perfectly.

Years later, Samantha received a letter from a state agency—not a penalty, not an audit, but a confirmation. Her account was in good standing. No action required.

She smiled and set it aside.

It wasn't the letter that mattered.

It was the absence of all the others.

Chapter 6

Scaling Without Fear: How AI Compliance Enables Unlimited Hiring, Expansion, and Growth

Growth has always been the paradox of business. The very actions that create opportunity—hiring more people, entering new markets, increasing revenue—also magnify compliance risk. Payroll obligations multiply with every employee. Sales tax exposure expands with every customer location. Employer regulations become more complex with every jurisdiction crossed. Historically, this meant that growth increased fragility. Businesses scaled revenue faster than their compliance systems, accumulating hidden liabilities that eventually surfaced as audits, penalties, lawsuits, or forced shutdowns. Artificial intelligence resolves this paradox by decoupling growth from risk, allowing businesses to scale indefinitely without losing control.

The central advantage of AI compliance systems is elasticity. Traditional compliance models are linear: more employees require more HR staff, more accountants, more payroll processing, and more oversight. AI compliance is exponential: one system enforces rules for ten employees as easily as it does for ten thousand. When a business hires a new employee, AI automatically determines jurisdictional requirements, tax registrations, labor law applicability, benefit eligibility, and reporting obligations. Nothing has to be rebuilt. The system simply extends its logic to new data points.

Multi-location and multi-state growth are where AI compliance becomes indispensable. Each state introduces unique payroll taxes, labor laws, filing schedules, and sales tax rules. Without automation, expansion requires legal research, registration paperwork, manual configuration, and ongoing monitoring. AI systems handle this automatically. The moment a hire is made or a sale occurs in a new jurisdiction, the system identifies applicable laws, initiates registrations where required, and enforces compliance going forward. Growth becomes operationally frictionless.

Remote work has further intensified compliance complexity. Employees may live in different states or countries than the company headquarters, triggering new tax and labor obligations. AI compliance platforms track employee location changes, remote work policies, and jurisdictional thresholds in real time. When a remote employee relocates, the system updates withholding, reporting, and labor law enforcement automatically. This eliminates one of the most common sources of accidental noncompliance in modern companies.

International expansion magnifies these challenges even further. Currency conversion, tax treaties, employment law differences, and reporting requirements historically required expensive global payroll providers and legal counsel. AI systems integrate international rules directly, applying country-specific compliance logic automatically. Businesses can hire globally without creating fragmented payroll infrastructures or exposing themselves to unknown liabilities.

From a strategic perspective, AI compliance changes how leaders think about growth. Hiring decisions are no longer delayed by fear of regulatory complexity. New markets are evaluated based on opportunity rather than administrative burden. Compliance ceases to be a bottleneck and becomes invisible infrastructure. This psychological shift alone has enormous economic value, allowing companies to move faster than competitors constrained by manual systems.

AI compliance also enables clean, scalable organizational structures. As businesses grow, consistency becomes critical. AI enforces standardized processes across departments, locations, and subsidiaries, ensuring that policies are applied uniformly. This consistency simplifies audits, improves internal controls, and increases trust among investors, lenders, and regulators. Most importantly, AI compliance enables sustainable growth. Businesses that grow without compliance eventually collapse under accumulated risk. AI-powered businesses grow with compliance embedded into every transaction, paycheck, and workforce decision. This creates organizations that are resilient, auditable, and structurally sound regardless of size.

In the AI-driven enterprise, growth no longer requires bravery. It requires architecture. When compliance is automated, expansion becomes a natural extension of operations rather than a leap into uncertainty. AI transforms scale from a liability into an advantage.

The Day Growth Stopped Being Scary

When Javier Molina founded his logistics technology company, growth was his obsession—and his fear. Every new contract meant new drivers, new warehouses, new states. Revenue climbed fast, but so did anxiety. Javier had seen too many companies implode not from lack of customers, but from compliance failures they never saw coming. He promised himself his company would be different, even if he didn't know how.

At first, the cracks were small. A delayed payroll registration in one state. A sales tax filing submitted late because the rules were different than expected. A remote employee who quietly moved across state lines without notifying HR. Each issue was "handled," but each one left a residue of doubt. Javier felt like he was sprinting across a frozen lake, never sure when the ice would give way.

The fear peaked when a potential enterprise client asked a simple question during due diligence: "Can you provide a complete, multi-state payroll and compliance audit trail for the last three years?" Javier realized he couldn't. Not cleanly. Not confidently. Growth, for the first time, felt like a threat.

That was the moment he committed to rebuilding his company's compliance infrastructure from the ground up using AI.

The implementation was unsettling. The system didn't flatter him. It exposed inconsistencies he had normalized, compliance risks that had gone unnoticed, and structural weaknesses that would have collapsed under further growth. But unlike the patchwork systems he had relied on before, the AI didn't just diagnose—it rebuilt.

As new hires came on, Javier noticed something strange: nothing broke. No extra meetings. No emergency emails. No last-minute filings. The AI system handled registrations, applied labor laws, updated payroll logic, and scheduled filings automatically. Growth no longer required coordination—it required permission. Then came the real test. A massive contract required Javier to hire across seven states in under sixty days. In the past, this would have been impossible without slowing down or cutting corners. This time, the AI system absorbed the expansion effortlessly. Each hire triggered automatic compliance workflows. Each state's rules were enforced invisibly. Payroll ran smoothly. Sales tax adjusted dynamically.

Javier waited for the chaos that never arrived.

Months later, the due diligence request came again—from an even larger partner. Javier sent the compliance report generated by the AI system. It showed every hire, every filing, every payment, every jurisdiction—clean, consistent, verifiable. The response came back in hours: "Approved."

As the company continued to scale, Javier noticed a profound shift in leadership meetings. Compliance was no longer discussed. Not because it was ignored, but because it was solved. Strategy conversations focused on opportunity, not avoidance. Hiring plans were ambitious again. Expansion felt exciting instead of dangerous.

Years later, Javier reflected on the moment growth stopped being scary. It wasn't when revenue stabilized. It wasn't when profits increased. It was when compliance became automatic—when the system made it impossible to fail quietly.

While competitors hesitated, burdened by fear and fragmented processes, his company moved freely, protected by an architecture that scaled as fast as ambition.

Growth, he realized, was never the problem.

Fear was.

And AI had removed it completely.

Chapter 7

Audit-Proof by Design: How AI Creates Permanent Compliance Memory and Defeats Enforcement Risk

Audits do not begin with wrongdoing; they begin with inconsistency. Government enforcement agencies rarely target businesses at random. They rely on algorithms, pattern detection, and anomaly scoring to identify organizations whose data does not align across payroll filings, tax reports, labor records, and financial statements. Historically, businesses failed audits not because they intended to evade compliance, but because their systems were fragmented, their records incomplete, and their documentation reconstructed after the fact. Artificial intelligence changes this dynamic entirely by creating what can be described as permanent compliance memory—an unbroken, time-stamped, verifiable record of every legally relevant action a business takes.

Traditional compliance operates backward. When an audit notice arrives, businesses scramble to gather documents, reconcile numbers, explain discrepancies, and recreate decisions made years earlier by people who may no longer work there. This reconstruction process introduces uncertainty, errors, and stress, often making situations worse rather than better. AI compliance systems eliminate reconstruction entirely. Every payroll calculation, tax filing, employee classification decision, benefit eligibility change, and jurisdictional adjustment is logged at the moment it occurs, preserved in its original context, and linked to the exact rules in force at that time.

This temporal intelligence is critical. Laws change constantly, and auditors evaluate actions based on the rules that existed when the action occurred—not current law. AI systems store historical regulatory logic alongside transactional data, allowing businesses to demonstrate not only what they did, but why it was correct under the law at that moment. This level of documentation is nearly impossible to achieve manually, yet it is precisely what enforcement agencies look for when determining intent and compliance quality.

Another powerful audit-defense feature of AI is cross-system reconciliation. Auditors often identify risk by comparing data across different filings. Payroll taxes must align with income tax filings. Employee counts must match benefit reports. Sales tax collections must reconcile with revenue figures. In manual environments, small discrepancies accumulate naturally as systems drift apart. AI compliance platforms prevent this drift by enforcing a single source of truth. Payroll, accounting, tax reporting, and HR data are synchronized continuously, eliminating the inconsistencies that trigger enforcement scrutiny.

AI also neutralizes one of the most dangerous audit accelerators: corrective filings. When businesses discover errors and submit amended returns without clear documentation, they often invite deeper investigation. AI systems reduce the need for amendments by validating filings before submission and flagging anomalies early. When corrections are necessary, the system documents the reason, the scope, and the remediation steps automatically, framing the correction as controlled compliance rather than reactive damage control.

From an enforcement perspective, AI-powered businesses behave differently. Their data is structured, consistent, and transparent. When audits occur, they are shorter, narrower, and less adversarial. Auditors can verify compliance quickly instead of probing for hidden issues. In many cases, AI-generated compliance logs satisfy inquiries before formal audits escalate.

Perhaps the most transformative effect of AI audit defense is cultural. When leadership knows that compliance is continuously documented and verifiable, decision-making improves. Shortcuts disappear. Risky ambiguity loses appeal. Compliance is no longer something to "manage later"; it is built into every operational choice. This cultural alignment further reduces enforcement exposure because behavior and documentation evolve together.

In the AI-enabled enterprise, audits lose their power. They become procedural reviews rather than existential threats. Businesses no longer fear what might be discovered because every action has already been evaluated, recorded, and justified in real time. Compliance stops being a defensive posture and becomes a permanent state.

Audit-proof organizations are not those that never make mistakes. They are those that never lose context. Artificial intelligence ensures that context is never lost.

Nothing to Explain

The audit notice arrived on a Tuesday afternoon, quiet and unremarkable, like so many government letters before it. But for Elena Fischer, it felt like time stopped.

She had built her healthcare staffing company over fifteen years, expanding slowly at first, then rapidly as demand exploded. Nurses, therapists, administrative staff—hundreds of employees across multiple states. The company had survived recessions, pandemics, and regulatory shifts that crushed competitors. Still, the word "audit" carried a weight that no amount of success could dissolve.

Elena remembered the last audit her previous company endured decades earlier. Boxes of documents. Sleepless nights. Arguments with accountants over numbers no one fully understood. Decisions reconstructed from memory. Explanations that sounded weaker the more they were repeated. That experience never left her.

This time, however, something was different.

Two years earlier, Elena had made a quiet decision to replace her patchwork compliance infrastructure with an AI-driven system. At the time, it felt excessive. Expensive. Almost paranoid. But she remembered how fragile compliance had once felt—how much depended on people remembering to do things correctly, consistently, forever.

When the auditors requested payroll records, Elena didn't panic. She logged into the system and granted read-only access.

When they asked for worker classification documentation, the AI produced a timeline for every role, showing classification logic, legal references, and decision points. Each change was justified. Each threshold was documented. When they questioned overtime calculations in one state, the system displayed labor law rules in effect during that period and showed how each paycheck complied. No explanations were needed. The math spoke for itself.

Days passed. Then weeks.

Elena waited for follow-up questions that never came.

Instead, the auditors requested fewer and fewer documents. Their tone shifted from investigative to confirmatory. What they were seeing didn't raise suspicion—it eliminated it. The company's data aligned across filings, agencies, and years. There were no contradictions to explore, no inconsistencies to unravel.

One auditor made an offhand comment during a call: "Your records are... unusually complete."

Elena smiled but said nothing.

Behind the scenes, the AI system continued to do what it always had. Logging. Reconciling. Preserving context. It didn't know an audit was happening. It didn't need to.

When the audit closed, the final letter was brief. No penalties. No adjustments. No recommendations. Just confirmation.

Elena sat in her office long after reading it, reflecting on the absence of fear she felt. Not relief—relief implied danger had existed. This was different. This was certainty.

Later that week, a fellow CEO called her in a panic. His company was facing a multi-state labor audit, and he didn't know where to begin. Elena listened quietly as he described missing records, conflicting reports, and employees who had long since left.

"You're going to be fine," she said gently, though she wasn't sure it was true.

After the call ended, Elena looked at her compliance dashboard. Every metric was green. Every system synchronized. Every action documented.

For the first time in her career, she realized something profound.

There was nothing left to explain.

The company didn't rely on memory, narratives, or excuses. It relied on truth—captured at the moment it occurred and preserved forever.

Audits had lost their power not because the rules were avoided, but because they were followed perfectly, automatically, and without exception. And in that silence—no penalties, no fear, no scrambling—Elena understood the true promise of artificial intelligence in business.

Not speed.

Not scale.

But certainty.

Chapter 8

When Compliance Becomes Strategy: Using AI to Turn Regulation Into Competitive Advantage

For most of business history, compliance has been treated as a defensive obligation—an unavoidable cost, a bureaucratic tax on growth, a necessary evil to survive regulation. Companies complied just enough to avoid penalties, audits, and lawsuits, but rarely more. Artificial intelligence fundamentally inverts this mindset. When compliance is automated, continuous, and mathematically enforced, it stops being a constraint and becomes a strategic asset. Businesses that embed AI compliance deeply into operations do not merely survive regulation; they outperform competitors because of it.

The first strategic advantage AI compliance creates is speed. In traditional organizations, expansion is slowed by regulatory uncertainty. Leadership hesitates before hiring, entering new states, launching products, or acquiring companies because compliance implications are unclear. AI eliminates this hesitation by making regulatory impact instantly visible and automatically managed. Decisions can be made faster because the system already understands the consequences and enforces the rules. Speed, in modern markets, is not optional—it is dominance.

The second advantage is credibility. Investors, lenders, partners, and enterprise customers increasingly evaluate companies based on operational maturity and regulatory posture. AI compliance systems produce clean, auditable, real-time records that signal discipline, transparency, and control. This lowers perceived risk and improves access to capital, partnerships, and large contracts. In many industries, compliance maturity is now a gating factor for growth, and AI-powered companies pass these gates effortlessly.

AI also enables strategic labor flexibility. Businesses can hire where talent exists rather than where compliance is easiest. Remote teams, cross-border employment, and dynamic workforce models become viable because AI enforces labor law automatically. This allows companies to optimize talent acquisition, compensation, and productivity without regulatory friction. Labor strategy becomes global rather than local.

From a financial standpoint, AI compliance improves forecasting and capital allocation. Because tax liabilities, payroll obligations, and regulatory costs are calculated continuously, leadership has a clearer picture of true margins and cash flow. Strategic decisions are made with accurate data rather than estimates. This precision compounds over time, producing structurally stronger businesses.

Perhaps most importantly, AI compliance changes organizational culture. When rules are enforced automatically, ethical behavior becomes the default rather than a personal burden. Employees and managers do not need to interpret gray areas or remember complex regulations. The system enforces boundaries consistently and impartially. This reduces internal conflict, improves trust, and aligns behavior across the organization.

In highly regulated industries, AI compliance becomes a moat. Competitors operating manually struggle with audits, penalties, and operational drag. AI-powered businesses move freely, protected by infrastructure rather than vigilance. Over time, this gap widens until compliance capability itself becomes a competitive barrier that others cannot easily cross.

In the AI-driven enterprise, compliance is no longer reactive. It is predictive, preventative, and strategic. Regulation stops being something to survive and becomes something to leverage. Businesses that understand this shift do not ask how to minimize compliance—they ask how to weaponize it.

The Company Regulators Trusted

When Margaret Liu took over as CEO of a mid-sized financial services firm, she inherited a company that looked successful on paper but fragile beneath the surface. Revenue was strong, employees were talented, and the market opportunity was enormous. But compliance was treated as an afterthought. Each department had its own processes, its own interpretations, its own "workarounds." Nothing was illegal, but nothing was unified.

Margaret had spent her early career inside regulatory agencies. She knew how enforcement really worked. She knew that regulators did not look for villains—they looked for inconsistency. And inconsistency, she could already see, was everywhere.

Instead of tightening policies or adding layers of oversight, Margaret made a controversial decision. She invested heavily in an AI-driven compliance infrastructure that touched every part of the business: payroll, sales tax, labor law, reporting, and audit defense. It was expensive. It slowed things down at first. People complained.

Then something unexpected happened. Meetings became shorter. Fewer questions needed clarification. Decisions that once required legal review were made confidently because the system already enforced the rules. Hiring accelerated. Expansion plans resumed.

Months later, the firm applied for a national partnership that required extensive regulatory vetting. Competitors spent weeks assembling documentation. Margaret granted reviewers access to the AI compliance dashboard.

The review was completed in days.

The feedback was striking: "Your compliance posture exceeds industry norms."

Soon, regulators began interacting with the firm differently. Requests were specific instead of broad. Audits were targeted instead of sweeping. The tone shifted from suspicion to trust.

Trust, Margaret knew, was the most valuable currency in regulated industries.

Years passed. Competitors struggled with penalties, public enforcement actions, and leadership turnover. Margaret's firm grew steadily, quietly, almost invisibly. It wasn't flashy. It was resilient.

One day, during a regulatory conference, a senior official made an offhand comment during a panel discussion. He referenced "a firm that demonstrates what modern compliance should look like." He didn't name the company, but Margaret recognized the description.

Her firm had become a benchmark.

Back at the office, she reflected on how counterintuitive the journey had been. While others treated compliance as a drag on innovation, she had treated it as infrastructure. While others tried to outrun regulation, she had embraced it fully—then automated it.

Employees no longer feared audits. Leadership no longer feared growth. The system enforced the rules so thoroughly that ethics became automatic.

Late one evening, Margaret walked through the empty office floors. Screens glowed quietly with dashboards tracking compliance metrics across states, departments, and years. Everything was green.

She realized something profound.

The company didn't just comply with the rules.

It embodied them.

And in doing so, it had achieved something far more powerful than profit. It had earned trust.

Not through promises.

Not through explanations.

But through systems that made wrongdoing impossible and compliance inevitable.

In a world where regulation was growing more complex and enforcement more automated, Margaret's company didn't resist the future.

It became the future.

And that, she knew, was the ultimate competitive advantage.

Chapter 9

Human Error Eliminated: How AI Replaces Fragile Processes With Permanent Precision

Every compliance failure in business history can be traced back to one root cause: human limitation. People forget. People misinterpret. People leave. People improvise. People make assumptions when systems are unclear. Traditional payroll, sales tax, and employer compliance frameworks were never designed to be perfect—they were designed to be "good enough" when managed by careful humans. But as regulation has expanded, deadlines multiplied, and jurisdictions overlapped, "good enough" has quietly become catastrophic. Artificial intelligence does not improve human compliance; it replaces the fragile parts entirely with permanent precision.

Manual compliance processes fail because they depend on memory and timing. Someone must remember to update a tax rate. Someone must remember that a filing deadline moved because of a holiday. Someone must remember that a remote employee relocated. Someone must remember that a benefit threshold was crossed. Each of these memories is a potential failure point. AI compliance systems remove memory from the equation. They monitor continuously, update automatically, and execute without pause. Compliance ceases to be an activity and becomes a condition.

Interpretation is another source of error. Labor law, tax regulation, and reporting requirements are filled with ambiguity, exceptions, and conditional logic. Human interpretation varies based on experience, fatigue, and incentive. AI does not interpret emotionally or contextually—it applies logic consistently. When rules are encoded into machine-readable frameworks, enforcement becomes uniform across time, departments, and leadership changes. This consistency is not merely efficient; it is defensible.

AI also eliminates the "handoff problem" that plagues compliance workflows. Payroll feeds accounting. Accounting feeds tax reporting. HR feeds payroll. Each handoff introduces delay and distortion. AI compliance platforms unify these domains into a single operational layer. Data flows instantly, without re-entry or reconciliation. The system does not forget what it already knows, and it does not lose information in translation.

Another hidden source of human error is corrective behavior. When humans discover mistakes, they often correct them quietly, adjusting spreadsheets or reissuing payments without documentation. These silent fixes create audit risk because records no longer reflect reality. AI systems log every correction with context, justification, and timestamp, preserving the narrative integrity of compliance. Nothing disappears. Nothing is overwritten. Everything is explainable.

Fatigue and volume amplify error. As businesses grow, the number of transactions, employees, and filings increases exponentially. Humans do not scale linearly under this pressure. AI does. Whether processing one payroll run or one million transactions, the system applies the same logic with the same accuracy. Scale does not degrade precision; it enhances it.

Perhaps the most dangerous human behavior in compliance is normalization of risk. When minor violations go unnoticed, they become accepted. Over time, shortcuts become policy. AI systems do not normalize deviation. They enforce rules without adaptation or rationalization. This prevents the slow drift toward noncompliance that destroys otherwise successful organizations.

By eliminating human error at the system level, AI does more than reduce penalties. It restores trust—in data, in decision-making, and in the organization itself. Leaders no longer wonder whether reports are accurate. Employees no longer fear accidental violations. Regulators no longer encounter inconsistencies. Compliance becomes boring, predictable, and silent.

In the AI-powered enterprise, perfection is not aspirational. It is operational. When human error is removed from compliance, the system no longer fails quietly. It simply does not fail at all.

The Mistake That Couldn't Happen

For nearly twenty years, Thomas Adler believed experience was his greatest asset. He had run payroll, accounting, and compliance operations for multiple companies. He knew the rules. He knew the exceptions. He knew which deadlines were "flexible" and which ones mattered. His confidence was built on repetition—on the idea that careful humans could outmaneuver complex systems.

That belief began to crack the year his company crossed five hundred employees.

At first, the errors were small. A payroll tax rate applied one quarter too late. A sales tax filing submitted under the wrong jurisdiction code. A benefit eligibility threshold crossed without notice. Each mistake was corrected. Each correction was undocumented. Each one felt harmless in isolation.

But Thomas noticed something unsettling: the mistakes were happening faster than they could be prevented. Every fix created new complexity. Every workaround required memory. Every memory depended on people who were already stretched thin.

Then came the call.

A regulator flagged inconsistencies between payroll filings and benefit reports. Nothing dramatic—yet. Just enough to trigger deeper review. Thomas stayed late, reconstructing decisions from emails, calendars, and conversations that no longer felt clear. He realized, for the first time, that the system depended entirely on people remembering what they had done months earlier.

That night, Thomas didn't sleep.

The company's leadership made a decision the following week. They implemented an AI compliance platform across payroll, sales tax, and employer reporting. Thomas felt threatened. The system didn't ask for his judgment. It didn't need his experience. It absorbed the rules and enforced them automatically.

At first, he looked for errors.

He expected the AI to miss nuances, overlook exceptions, or misapply thresholds. It didn't. It flagged issues before they happened. It prevented filings that would have been incorrect. It corrected classifications automatically. It logged every action with context he never could have reconstructed himself.

Weeks passed. Then months.

Thomas noticed something he hadn't felt in years: calm.

There were no emergency corrections. No frantic reconciliations. No late-night explanations. The system didn't rely on him to remember. It remembered everything itself.

Then the regulator followed up.

This time, Thomas didn't scramble. He granted access.

The audit moved quickly. Painfully efficiently. Every question had an answer already embedded in the system. Every inconsistency had been prevented before it existed. There was nothing to explain because nothing had gone wrong.

When the audit closed, the regulator made a brief comment: "Your data integrity is unusually strong."

Thomas leaned back in his chair, stunned.

He realized something profound—and uncomfortable.

The system no longer needed him to prevent mistakes.

It made mistakes impossible.

For the first time in his career, Thomas understood that experience had limits. Memory decayed. Judgment varied. Fatigue crept in. But logic, once encoded, did not forget.

As the company continued to grow, Thomas's role changed. He stopped fixing errors and started analyzing strategy. He stopped guarding compliance and started trusting it. The system handled perfection. He handled vision.

One afternoon, a junior analyst asked him how the company avoided compliance issues so effectively.

Thomas paused, then smiled.

"We don't avoid mistakes," he said. "We built a system where they can't happen."

And in that moment, he understood that the future of compliance was not smarter people.

It was smarter systems.

Systems that didn't rely on vigilance.

Systems that didn't rely on memory.

Systems that didn't rely on hope.

Just truth, enforced automatically—forever.

Chapter 10

The Autonomous Compliance Enterprise: When Business Runs Itself

The ultimate destination of AI payroll, sales tax, and employer compliance is not efficiency—it is autonomy. In the autonomous compliance enterprise, regulation is no longer managed, monitored, or supervised. It is executed automatically as an inherent property of the organization's operating system. This represents a structural evolution in how businesses exist. Just as electricity became invisible infrastructure rather than a daily concern, compliance becomes embedded, ambient, and unavoidable. The business runs itself within the boundaries of law by default.

Autonomous compliance emerges when AI systems no longer require human triggers to act. Payroll calculations initiate automatically as labor is performed. Tax liabilities are reserved the moment revenue is earned. Filings are prepared continuously rather than episodically. Reporting is generated dynamically rather than reactively. No one presses a button. No one remembers a deadline. Compliance occurs because the system is architected to make any other outcome impossible. This autonomy is achieved through layered intelligence. At the base layer, transactional AI records every legally relevant action—hours worked, wages paid, sales completed, benefits accrued. Above that, regulatory intelligence interprets applicable law in real time, adjusting logic as rules evolve. Above that, execution intelligence files, pays, reports, and reconciles automatically. At the top, audit intelligence preserves historical context, ensuring that every action remains defensible forever. Together, these layers form a closed-loop compliance system with no external dependencies.

One of the most powerful implications of autonomous compliance is organizational continuity. Traditional compliance systems degrade over time as staff turnover, knowledge is lost, and processes drift. Autonomous systems do not degrade. They retain memory, logic, and enforcement capacity regardless of personnel changes. A company can replace its entire leadership team without losing compliance integrity. This continuity is unprecedented in business history.

Autonomy also eliminates the final source of risk: discretion. Many compliance failures occur when individuals are allowed to decide when rules matter. AI removes discretion from enforcement while preserving discretion for strategy. Humans decide what the business should do. AI ensures it is done legally. This division of responsibility creates clarity, accountability, and safety. From a regulatory perspective, autonomous enterprises are fundamentally different entities.

They do not hide, resist, or evade oversight. Their systems generate transparent, verifiable data by design. Regulators interact with these businesses not as suspects, but as stable participants in the economic system. Over time, this may reshape enforcement models entirely.

The autonomous compliance enterprise is not a vision of the future—it is a requirement for scale in a world where regulation, complexity, and enforcement are accelerating simultaneously. Businesses that do not adopt autonomy will face compounding risk. Businesses that do will operate freely within a legal framework enforced automatically and continuously.

At this stage, compliance disappears—not because it is ignored, but because it is complete. What remains is a business that moves faster, grows safely, and endures.

The Company That Never Slept and Never Forgot

No one at Axiom Industries remembered the last time someone "ran compliance."

There was no department for it anymore. No emergency meetings. No calendar reminders. No whispered conversations about deadlines or filings. Compliance wasn't a function. It was a condition. Years earlier, Axiom had been like every other company—ambitious, fast-moving, and quietly fragile. Payroll ran through vendors. Sales tax was tracked in spreadsheets. Employer filings were managed by people who understood the rules just well enough to keep things moving. Growth was celebrated publicly and feared privately.

The turning point came after a minor incident—a filing error that was caught early but exposed something unsettling. No one could explain exactly how the system worked. It functioned because people compensated for its weaknesses instinctively. Knowledge lived in habits, not architecture.

That realization changed everything.

Axiom rebuilt itself from the inside out, replacing human-dependent compliance with autonomous systems powered by artificial intelligence. At first, it felt excessive. The system watched everything. Recorded everything. Enforced everything. It didn't ask for approval. It didn't need reminders.

Then the company grew.

And nothing broke.

New hires triggered automatic compliance workflows. New markets initiated registrations without discussion. Payroll executed flawlessly. Taxes were calculated, filed, and paid without intervention. Employees never worried about pay accuracy. Leadership never worried about penalties.

One night, long after the office had emptied, the CEO walked through the building. Screens glowed softly in the dark—dashboards tracking compliance across time zones, jurisdictions, and years. The system was working. It always was.

An audit came and went without disruption. A regulator requested access, reviewed the system, and closed the case in record time. No explanations were needed. No defenses mounted.

The company didn't respond to compliance.

It embodied it.

As competitors stumbled under the weight of complexity, Axiom expanded effortlessly. They hired where talent existed. They sold where opportunity appeared. They scaled without fear.

Years later, during a leadership transition, the outgoing CEO made a quiet observation to her successor.

"This company doesn't rely on people to do the right thing," she said. "It makes the right thing inevitable."

The successor nodded, understanding immediately.

The company never slept. It never forgot. It never improvised.

It simply ran—within the law, within reason, within control.

And in a world growing more complex by the day, that autonomy wasn't just an advantage.

It was survival.

Final Thoughts

The End of Compliance Fear

For most business owners, payroll, sales tax, and employer compliance have never felt like systems—they have felt like threats. Invisible deadlines, shifting regulations, conflicting advice, and punitive enforcement created an environment where fear quietly shaped decisions. Hiring was delayed. Expansion was avoided. Innovation slowed. Not because opportunity was lacking, but because compliance uncertainty made progress feel dangerous. This book has shown that this fear was never inevitable. It was structural. And structure can be rebuilt.

Artificial intelligence does not merely improve compliance efficiency; it eliminates the conditions that create compliance anxiety in the first place. When rules are enforced automatically, continuously, and without discretion, businesses no longer need to rely on vigilance, memory, or heroics. Compliance stops being something you *do* and becomes something you *are*. This is the defining shift of the AI-powered enterprise. Throughout this book, you have seen how payroll transforms from a recurring risk into a real-time intelligence system. Every hour worked, every dollar paid, and every tax withheld becomes a verified data point, aligned with current law and preserved permanently. You have seen how sales tax automation turns every transaction into a compliant legal event, regardless of jurisdiction or scale. You have seen how employer compliance—once fragmented across HR, payroll, legal, and accounting—becomes unified under a single enforcement logic that never forgets and never improvises.

More importantly, you have seen how these systems change behavior. When compliance is automated, shortcuts disappear. Risk normalization stops. Decision-making improves. Leaders stop asking whether they *can* grow safely and start asking how fast they *should*. The psychological tax of compliance vanishes, replaced by confidence rooted in infrastructure rather than hope.

This book is not about replacing professionals. It is about freeing them. Accountants, payroll specialists, HR leaders, and executives become strategists instead of firefighters. Time once spent fixing mistakes is redirected toward optimization, planning, and growth. AI does not remove human judgment—it removes human fragility from places where it never belonged.

Perhaps the most profound lesson is this: compliance is no longer a cost center. It is a competitive advantage. Businesses that adopt AI-powered compliance systems operate faster, scale safer, and attract more trust from regulators, partners, investors, and employees. Over time, this advantage compounds. Companies without automation accumulate invisible risk. Companies with it accumulate resilience.

As regulation grows more complex and enforcement becomes increasingly algorithmic, manual compliance will not merely be inefficient—it will be unsustainable. The future belongs to autonomous compliance enterprises that embed law directly into operations, making violations statistically improbable and audits procedurally irrelevant.

If there is one truth to carry forward from this book, it is this: **The safest businesses are not the most careful ones. They are the most automated ones.**

When compliance becomes invisible, growth becomes inevitable.

www.ingramcontent.com/pod-product-compliance
Ingram Content Group UK Ltd.
Pitfield, Milton Keynes, MK11 3LW, UK
UKHW020156290926
15471UKWH00005B/909

9 798295 593369